Amy Ruth

Lerner Publications Company
Minneapolis

*This book is dedicated with love and thanks
to my sister, who has always played
Sense to my Sensibility.*

A note on the front cover image: The cover image, thought to be a portrait of Jane Austen (but never authenticated as such), is taken from a photogravure of a painting by an unknown artist. The painting is said to have been owned for many years by Colonel Austen of Kippington, and later by Jane Austen's grandnephew. It has since passed to a private collector.

A&E and **BIOGRAPHY** are trademarks of the A&E Television Networks, registered in the United States and other countries.

Some of the people profiled in this series have also been featured in A&E's acclaimed BIOGRAPHY series, which is available on videocassette from A&E Home Video. Call 1-800-423-1212 to order.

Lerner Publications Company
A division of Lerner Publishing Group
241 First Avenue North
Minneapolis, MN 55401 U.S.A.

Website address: www.lernerbooks.com

Library of Congress Cataloging-in-Publication Data

Ruth, Amy.
    Jane Austen / by Amy Ruth.
        p.   cm. — (A&E biography)
    Includes bibliographical references and index.
    ISBN 0-8225-4992-1 (lib. bdg. : alk. paper)
    1. Austen, Jane, 1775–1817—Juvenile literature. 2. Novelists,
English—19th century—Biography—Juvenile literature. [1. Austen, Jane,
1775–1817. 2. Authors, English. 3. Women—Biography.] I. Title.
II. Series.
PR4036.R88   2001
823'.7—dc21   00-009315

Manufactured in the United States of America
1 2 3 4 5 6 – JR – 06 05 04 03 02 01

CONTENTS

As a child, Jane enjoyed the quiet beauty of the English countryside and spent much of her time outdoors.

Chapter **ONE**

JANE

IN THE HAZY QUIET OF A SUMMER EVENING IN **1782,** six-year-old Jane Austen and her younger brother, Charles, waited on a country lane for their sister, Cassandra. Jane was always anxious when Cassandra traveled from their home in Steventon, a small village in southern England, to visit relatives in the city of Bath. Jane couldn't bear to be apart from her older sister.

This time, Jane could not wait passively at home for Cassandra's return. While her mother was busy, Jane slipped out of the house, dragging her three-year-old brother, Charles, behind her. They walked through the quiet village and along a dusty lane next to meadows and woods. After reaching the main road, Jane and

Charles listened for the rattling of carriage wheels and the clip-clop of horses' hooves.

Their father, Reverend George Austen, had gone to collect Cassandra. Returning to Steventon, he was surprised to see his two youngest children so far from home without an adult chaperone.

Throughout her life, Jane Austen would continue to surprise and delight her family with her imagination, intelligence, sharp wit, and lively personality. An outgoing person who spent most of her time with family, Jane's life was full of contrasts. Unmarried, Jane often lingered on the outskirts of social activity. Still, she challenged the conventional manners that limited what women and girls could do. As the daughter of a country minister, Jane was not wealthy, but she had enough social connections to become a keen observer of English country life. While she spent most of her time with her family, her writing examined the complexity of human nature.

Although Jane led a full life, she was misunderstood by some family members. One of her nephews wrote, "Of events her life was singularly barren: few changes and no great crisis ever broke the smooth current of its course." After her death, her brother Henry tried to portray her as sweet and meek, a lonely spinster. In fact, Jane loved to dance, flirt, and gossip, and she had several admirers. She had a sharp tongue and often made clever but unkind remarks about people she knew.

Jane lived during a time of great social and political change, including wars between America and Great Britain and France and Great Britain. Yet, in the six novels she published, she chose to portray the world that lay just beyond her front door. She described her focus as "the little bit (two inches wide) of ivory on which I work."

Jane wrote about the lives of middle- and upper-class families in rural England in a new style of writing, called domestic realism, that became popular across the world. Although her writing received little distinction during her lifetime, Jane Austen secured a place in history as one of the great female novelists.

THE AUSTEN FAMILY

Born on December 16, 1775, Jane Austen was the seventh of eight children—older siblings James, George, Edward, Henry, Cassandra, and Francis, and a younger brother, Charles. In a letter announcing Jane's birth, the Rev. Austen wrote, "We now have another girl, a present plaything for her sister Cassy and a future companion." Jane's parents, George and Cassandra, were related to the Knight family, who owned much of the land around Steventon. A village tucked into a valley in the county of Hampshire, Steventon was home to villagers who were mainly farm laborers.

Thomas Knight, the head of the family, did not live in the area but rented out the family's grand Steventon Manor. He allowed the Rev. Austen to earn his living as the rector, or minister, for Steventon and the nearby village of Deane. As the rector, the Rev. Austen could live in the Steventon Rectory and collect income from rented church lands.

During Jane's lifetime, Great Britain was governed by a rigid class structure. Families in the aristocracy, or upper class, inherited fortunes, property, and titles of nobility. They also held important government positions. The middle class was composed of professionals like the Rev. Austen, people who worked as clergy, lawyers, teachers, doctors, and merchants. The lower classes—laborers and servants—worked for the upper and middle classes.

Like her brothers and sister before her, Jane spent almost the first two years of her life with a wet nurse. This woman, who lived in the village, fed and cared for Jane. It was common for families to rely on others to care for their babies until the children were toilet trained and could speak a little. All but one of the Austen children were physically healthy. This was remarkable, since more than half of all children at the time died of disease or accidents before their second birthday. George Austen, the second oldest son, was probably physically and mentally challenged. He was cared for by village families his whole life.

A FULL HOUSE

The Austens were overjoyed by Jane's birth, even though Steventon Rectory was already bursting at the

The Reverend George Austen was a loving father. He shared Jane's love of reading and often brought home new books for the family to read.

seams. The solid, three-storied house had a large kitchen, roomy parlors, a study, and ten bedrooms, but it was home to as many as fifteen people at a time. The Rev. Austen opened a boarding school to earn extra money, and several pupils lived in the attic. The Rev. Austen held classes in his study, which overlooked the gardens behind the house.

Keeping the children fed, washed, and clothed was exhausting work, not only because there were so many of them, but because all household tasks were done by hand. Water was retrieved from an outside pump and lugged inside for cooking and washing. Preparing food kept the kitchen boiling over with activity. All but the poorest families hired servants to help with the time-consuming work.

Somewhat isolated in the remote village, the Austens

Cassandra Leigh Austen, Jane's mother, came from a higher social rank than her husband. Although they did not have much money, Jane's parents provided a loving home.

lived in a self-contained world. They provided their own amusement and were united by strong bonds of loyalty. Like most country families, the Austens produced almost all the food they ate. Mrs. Austen raised chickens, turkeys, and geese, calling them her "riches." She tended a large vegetable garden and was known throughout the village for her strawberries. With the help of maids, she ran an organized and efficient dairy, baked bread, pickled vegetables, and brewed beer and wine. From the sheep and the pigs her husband raised, Mrs. Austen prepared mutton, bacon, and ham. The Austen boys were fond of hunting and often supplied game for the supper table.

Because Mrs. Austen was preoccupied with homemaking, Cassandra often looked after Jane. Jane greatly admired her sister, who was three years older.

The Rev. Austen's prediction that his two daughters would be companions quickly became true.

From time to time, the Austens socialized with other local families. In the nearby town of Dummer, the Terry family's thirteen children were playmates of the Austens. The friendly Digweed family, with four boys close in age to the Austen children, rented Steventon Manor. When winter's cold and snow kept families inside, they often gathered for dinner and dancing.

In May 1779, when Jane was three, the family supporter, Thomas Knight, visited Steventon with his new wife, Catherine. They liked Jane's twelve-year-old brother Edward so much they asked him to join them on their travels. The next month, Mrs. Austen gave birth to her eighth child, Charles. Within two weeks of Charles's birth, fourteen-year-old James, the oldest son, left to study at St. John's College in Oxford.

Edward was not the only Austen to receive attention from a wealthy relative. Mrs. Austen's sister, Jane Leigh Cooper, lived in Bath with her husband, Dr. Edward Cooper. The couple had a daughter, Jane, who was about Cassandra's age. Soon Cassandra was traveling to Bath for extended visits with her cousin.

The Rev. and Mrs. Austen were good-natured and affectionate parents. They provided a cheerful, comfortable home for their children. Jane enjoyed listening to the Rev. Austen read aloud from novels and books of poetry. And there were always jokes, games, and laughter in the Austen household.

At the age of seven, Jane left her beloved Steventon to attend a girls' school in Oxford, England.

Chapter **TWO**

AWAY TO SCHOOL

FROM THE TIME SHE WAS A YOUNG GIRL, JANE FOUND comfort in Steventon's natural beauty. She delighted in the green hills sloping toward thick woods and the meadows covered with yellow cowslips. In Steventon, as in other rural villages, life advanced according to nature's timetable, which determined when to work and when to pause to enjoy life's pleasures. To Jane, this steady and predictable rhythm was like a second heartbeat. She and Cassandra spent as much time outdoors as possible, walking, playing, and helping their mother in the garden.

By the time Jane was seven, she and Cassandra had become constant playmates, loyal friends, and confidantes. They were so close, in fact, that their mother once remarked, "If Cassandra were going to have her head cut off, Jane would insist on sharing the fate." When the Austens considered sending Cassandra to boarding school with her cousin Jane Cooper, Jane begged to go, too. She would rather be away from home with Cassandra than stay in her beloved Steventon without her.

Although it was unusual to send a girl as young as seven away to school, the Austens gave in to Jane's pleas. She, Cassandra, and Jane Cooper would go to Oxford, where Dr. Cooper's sister, Ann Cawley, operated a girls' school.

A Girl's Education

Small boarding schools such as the Rev. Austen's, which prepared boys to attend universities, were common in England during the 1700s. Educating girls, however, was generally considered a waste of time and money. Women didn't need to be able to read Latin or understand philosophy to run a household and raise children. Many people believed that women were less intelligent than men and could not learn subjects such as math and science. Some authors even claimed that women could hurt themselves by pursuing an education. The year before Jane was born, a popular parenting book warned that if a girl made the mistake of acquiring knowledge, she should "keep it a profound secret, especially from men." Another parenting book declared, "Wit is a very desirable quality in a man . . . . In women I am sure it is always to be feared."

Most girls were educated at home. Rich families hired governesses and tutors to teach music, drawing, foreign languages, and social graces such as dancing. Less wealthy parents taught their own children to read, write, and do math. Poor children usually had to work and received little schooling.

Like other girls, Jane and Cassandra learned how to run an efficient household. Mrs. Austen taught her daughters to sew and embroider, supervised their penmanship, and showed them how to cook, tend a vegetable garden, and supervise servants. For many parents, this would have been enough education for a girl. But the Austens were different. They recognized and encouraged their daughters' intelligence.

SCHOOL AND SICKNESS

The girls arrived in Oxford in the spring of 1783. Soon after, Mrs. Cawley moved her school to Southampton, a port city about twenty-five miles south of Steventon. The war with the American colonies was almost over, and British troops were returning home. The soldiers brought with them a deadly fever. Many residents of Southampton became infected, including Cassandra and Jane. While Cassandra's case was mild, Jane grew sicker and sicker. Jane Cooper wrote to her parents in Bath about her cousins' illness, and Mrs. Cooper and Mrs. Austen rushed to the school. Mrs. Cooper took her daughter home immediately, but Jane Austen was too sick to travel. Finally, she recovered and was able to go home. Jane's aunt, Mrs. Cooper, was not so lucky. She herself became sick and died shortly after returning home to Bath.

While Jane was at school, her brother Edward had gone to live with the wealthy Knight family at Godmersham, their estate in Kent. The Knights, who had no children of their own, wanted to adopt Edward and make him their heir. It was a difficult decision, but the Austens agreed to the adoption. They knew that the Knights could give Edward more opportunities and financial security than they could.

Adopted by rich relatives, Edward Austen remained close to his siblings and birth parents.

For the next year, Cassandra and Jane remained at home, taking lessons from their father. Unlike most fathers of the time, the Rev. Austen did not restrict his daughters' reading. Choosing from the Rev. Austen's library of almost five hundred books, Jane read many novels with racy plots and characters, including mistresses and drunken men. She also read serious literature—plays, poetry, historical and travel accounts, and magazines. She enjoyed plays by William Shakespeare and the novels of Samuel Johnson and Henry Fielding, two important eighteenth-century writers.

Jane's brother Henry remarked that Jane was an eager reader with an incredible memory. "It is difficult to say at what age she was not intimately acquainted with the merits and defects of the best essays and novels in the English language," he wrote.

In the spring of 1785, Cassandra and Jane were sent to another boarding school with their cousin Jane. The Abbey School in Reading, a town twenty-six miles north of Steventon, had an excellent reputation. Operated by an Englishwoman who called herself Madame La Tournelle, the Abbey School provided a comfortable home away from home. Students attended classes only in the morning, with the afternoons free to do as they wished.

Cassandra and Jane stayed at the Abbey School for almost two years. The Austens brought them home for good in December 1787. It is likely that the Rev. Austen could no longer afford the school's fees. In

Cassandra and Jane attended the Abbey School in Reading, above, for almost two years, but they received most of their education at home.

addition, the quality of his daughters' education probably concerned him. Madame La Tournelle's loose attitude was not altogether proper. The headmistress allowed teachers to eat breakfast with curlers in their hair and often rushed through morning prayers.

With Jane and Cassandra back home, the Rev. Austen relied on his wife and a few local schoolmasters to teach them. Cassandra was a talented artist who also enjoyed growing plants and flowers. Jane learned to play the piano and became an accomplished musician.

Twelve-year-old Jane quickly slipped back into the familiar rhythm of life at Steventon Rectory. Surrounded by the people and places she loved, she took up her pen and began to compete with her mother and her brother James for the title of "poet of the family."

ENGLAND IN JANE AUSTEN'S TIME

Between 1714 and 1830, known as the Georgian period, kings George I, George II, George III, and George IV ruled England. For many people, it was a time of hope and prosperity. Europe experienced a temporary relief from epidemics of disease. The farming of new crops, including potatoes, led to bountiful food production.

While England was still mostly an agricultural country, the Industrial Revolution began to transform the nation in the 1760s. Factories churned out textiles, coal, iron, and other manufactured products. English exports and trade flourished. At the same time, landowners experimented with improved farming techniques. They enclosed many small, scattered tracts of land into larger, unified fields, separated by hedges.

Most people lived in the countryside. Poor families did not own the land they farmed. Children worked alongside adults to earn more money for the family. Poor women and children often worked as household servants for very low wages. As a result, families like the Austens could afford several servants.

Unlike the workers, middle- and upper-class people like the Austens had leisure time to pursue hobbies. Gardening and landscaping became popular. People enjoyed picnics, musical concerts, and sports. Organized social activities, such as dances in public "assembly rooms," became more common.

In this world, class distinctions and strict rules of conduct were important. Social status was determined not by money but by family lineage. Men's and women's roles were also clearly defined. Men worked or inherited money and property. Women did not work outside the home. They could not vote or own property. For lower-class women and girls, life was never-ending labor, while middle- and upper-class girls prepared only to become wives and mothers. Women ran the household and made sure the children received proper moral instruction.

While growing up at the Steventon Rectory, above, *Jane entertained her family by reading the short stories and poems she wrote.*

Chapter **THREE**

"UNLIKE A GIRL OF TWELVE"

LIKE THE BOISTEROUS TALK OF THE BOYS WHO FILLED Steventon Rectory, Jane's early writings were packed with exaggerations, absurd humor, and crude jokes. She wound her plots around jilted lovers, drunkenness, public fights, and other scandalous behavior. Her characters were buffoons, thieves, and ignorant fools. They rarely escaped horrible and ridiculous fates, including murders, fainting fits, and violent accidents. Jane's family loved to hear her read her hilarious stories.

Jane's comical plots and heroes weren't just entertaining. They also poked fun at popular novels of the time. When Jane began to write, British readers were devouring so-called sentimental novels. These novels relied on unrealistic plots and coincidences to tell a story. Characters were either virtuous or evil. But Jane knew that real people weren't all good or all bad. In sentimental novels, the heroines were upset easily and fainted often. These characters were nothing like the women Jane knew. The women in her life were strong and independent. For example, her aunt Philadelphia Austen Hancock had traveled alone to India. Philadelphia's daughter, Eliza, was educated in Europe and later married a French count. Some of Jane's female relatives were published authors, including Mrs. Austen's cousin, Cassandra Cooke, who had written a historical novel.

Sentimental novels could be fun to read, but Jane had no patience for characters—real or imagined—who had little sense. In her story "Edgar and Emma," Jane created a spoof of such a character. Emma is so distraught when she learns that her beloved Edgar will not visit that she runs to her bedroom. There she "continued in tears the remainder of her Life."

Jane also disliked women who were more concerned about money than love. In "Amelia Webster," Jane made fun of the stiff and unromantic process of finding a rich husband—the likely plot of a sentimental novel. The six characters barely knew each other before Jane had them paired off and married. In a particularly absurd twist, one man declares, "I saw you thro' a telescope & was so struck by your Charms that from that time to this I have not tasted human food."

COUSIN ELIZA

While the novels of the time inspired Jane, the comings and goings at Steventon Rectory also provided material for the budding writer. In December 1787, the month Jane turned twelve, the Austens celebrated the Christmas holiday with Aunt Philadelphia, her daughter, Eliza, and Eliza's baby son, Hastings. Already a busy place, Steventon Rectory grew even livelier when cousin Eliza visited. Her life was almost as exciting as Jane's fiction.

Fourteen years older than Jane, the beautiful and vivacious Eliza mesmerized the Austen household with descriptions of her husband's castles and the lavish parties they attended. With their shared love of storytelling, she and Jane became especially close.

Like all the Austens, Eliza loved music, literature, and drama. The cousins had a great time organizing theatrical performances. They built and painted a stage in the barn, and Eliza provided colorful costumes. The group also had help from a writer, Egerton Brydges, who lived in nearby Deane village. Years later, Brydges described Jane as "fair and handsome, slight and elegant, but with cheeks a little too full."

The amateur acting troupe held several performances over the holidays and invited friends from Steventon and surrounding villages. Jane was probably too young to be given a part, but she was surely watching attentively. And she was listening. From the works of various playwrights, she was

Jane was inspired by her beautiful and adventurous cousin Eliza.

learning how to craft witty dialogue for her stories.

In the summer of 1788, the Austens visited relatives in Kent and London. Jane knew better than to share her outrageous stories outside the immediate family circle. Most people would not approve of a clever girl whose head was jammed with sarcastic tales. But Jane could not hide her wit and intelligence. Mrs. Austen's niece, Philadelphia Walter, took an immediate dislike to Jane. She wrote to her brother, "The youngest is . . . not at all pretty and . . . unlike a girl of twelve."

MISCHIEVOUS CHARACTERS

The Austens' trip included what was probably Jane's first visit to London. The city inspired several stories when she returned home. Jane set *The Beautifull Cassandra* in London. The main character is the mischievous sixteen-year-old Cassandra, whose mother is a hatmaker. Cassandra admires her mother's newest creation and decides to show it off. She sets out alone on a seven-hour walk, misbehaving at every turn. After flirting with a man she has just met, "She then proceeded to a Pastry-cooks where she devoured six ices, refused to pay for them, knocked down the Pastry Cook & walked away."

In her short novel *Henry and Eliza*, named for her brother and cousin, Jane invented another unladylike heroine. Eliza steals money from her adopted parents

After visiting London, Jane set some of her stories in the bustling city, which lay along the banks of the Thames River, above.

Jane used simple writing tools similar to these.

and runs away to France with her lover, who is engaged to another woman. In France, Eliza has two children, who partially eat her alive before she is captured and imprisoned in England.

GOOD FRIENDS

Jane understood that in real life she had to behave like a proper lady. But social expectations did not limit her vivid imagination. She said on paper what she could not say out loud.

Among the Steventon neighbors, Jane did find

friends who enjoyed the same kinds of activities as she did. The Austens' closest neighbors were the Lefroys, who lived at Ashe Rectory. The Rev. Isaac Lefroy, his wife, and their two children became friendly with the Austens. Fourteen-year-old Jane regularly walked the two miles to the Lefroys' home to see Mrs. Anne Lefroy. Like Jane, Mrs. Lefroy loved music and literature.

Other new friends included the Lloyd family, who rented the Deane parsonage. Mrs. Lloyd was a widow with two daughters—Mary, who was in her early twenties, and Martha, who was in her late teens. In 1789 the Bigg family—with three teenage daughters, Alethea, Elizabeth, and Catherine, and a son, Harris—moved into Manydown Park, a large manor home four miles from Deane. Mr. Bigg had inherited the estate.

The Lloyd and Bigg sisters often joined the Austen girls on walks in the country or on shopping trips to Basingstoke, another nearby town. When the girls were together, Steventon and Deane rectories and Manydown Park rang with squeals of laughter and giddy gossip. Jane was especially fascinated by the scandalous stories the Lloyd sisters told about their grandmother, Mrs. Craven. She seduced wealthy men and was so cruel to her daughters, including Mary and Martha's mother, that they ran away from home.

Although Jane was a cynical writer, she dreamed of love and marriage. When she was fifteen, she made pretend entries in the Steventon parish register, proclaiming her marriage to two imaginary men, "Henry Frederic Howard Fitzwilliam of London" and "Edmund Arthur William Mortimer."

New friends and romantic fantasies may have prompted Jane to write *Love and Freindship* [sic] in the summer of 1790. Written in the form of letters, *Love and Freindship* was Jane's longest work to date. In it, she continued her attack on the sentimental novel. In one scene, she exaggerated the common female ploy of fainting to gain a man's attention. A dying mother tells her daughter, "My beloved Laura . . . take warning from my unhappy End & . . . beware of fainting fits. One fatal swoon has cost me my life. Beware of swoons, dear Laura."

Jane's brother Francis eventually became a well-respected admiral in the British navy.

Jane continued to entertain her family with her stories. For her brother Francis, who had gone to sea as a naval midshipman, Jane composed two stories: "The Adventures of Mr. Harley," featuring the unfortunate Mr. Harley, who forgets he is married, and the raunchy "Jack & Alice." Jane must have laughed out loud as she created a country village filled with girls who were so "Envious, Spitefull & Malicious . . . [and] short, fat, and disagreeable" that they poisoned one another and started bar fights with the town's drunks and gamblers.

The Rev. and Mrs. Austen did not record what they thought of their daughter's wild stories. But they did encourage her writing. In one of the notebooks the Rev. Austen gave to Jane, he wrote, "Effusions of Fancy by a very Young Lady Consisting of Tales in a Style entirely new."

Only about one hundred of the many letters Jane wrote to her sister, Cassandra, have survived. They provide valuable insights into Jane's life.

Chapter FOUR

"EVERY THING CAME FINISHED FROM HER PEN"

THAT JANE STEPPED UP HER LITERARY ACTIVITIES ONCE the rectory emptied of brothers and pupils is not a co-incidence. In 1791 the Rev. Austen had reduced the number of pupils he took in at the rectory. And with Charles Austen's departure for the Royal Naval Academy, all the Austen boys had left home. With fewer students and no brothers in the house, Jane and Cassandra could claim an unused room next to their bedroom as their own quiet place to work.

The new dressing room, as they called it, needed a face-lift. Jane and Cassandra had the bookshelves painted to match the carpet and covered the walls with pretty blue wallpaper. The sisters hung matching blue-and-white checked curtains.

In this private space, Jane wrote stories and poems or played the piano while Cassandra sketched or painted. The girls also read and wrote letters, practiced their French and Italian, and did needlework.

In July 1791, the Austens escorted Charles to the Naval Academy in Portsmouth and took a brief seaside holiday there. Cousin Eliza had speculated that her teenage cousins might find husbands among the throngs of naval officers in Portsmouth. Instead, the town inspired Jane to write. She was growing more and more disgusted with the "good-for-nothing" soldiers, kings, and other men in the history books she read. She also noticed that there were "hardly any women at all." She decided to write her own history of England. She asked Cassandra to illustrate it.

Jane's History

Jane's essay was a parody of Oliver Goldsmith's *The History of England*. Goldsmith, a famous poet, playwright, and novelist who died a year before Jane was born, published his immense four-volume textbook in 1771. It was later condensed into one volume. Having studied her father's copy as a schoolgirl, Jane was familiar with Goldsmith's history. She resented the way he glossed over important details and failed to include dates and facts. Jane thought that history books, like novels, should reflect reality.

In her own *The History of England*, Jane humorously summed up the reigns of kings and queens. She

Cassandra drew the illustrations for Jane's version of The History of England.

warned her reader: "There will be very few dates in this History."

According to Jane's fanciful history, Henry V "was burnt alive, but I forget what for." Of Edward IV, she wrote, "This monarch was famous . . . for his undaunted Behavior in marrying one Woman while he was engaged to another." Regarding Henry VII, Jane observed, "His Majesty died & was succeeded by his son Henry whose only merit was his not being *quite* so bad as his daughter Elizabeth."

As Jane wrote, Cassandra drew unflattering miniature portraits of Britain's royalty. She painted queens with sour-looking expressions and kings dressed in rags. Others looked like servants or wore ridiculous hats. Some even looked like children.

As the Austen children grew up, wedding bells began ringing at Steventon. Edward Austen Knight married the wealthy and beautiful Elizabeth Bridges in December 1791. The following year, James married Anne Mathew.

Although James's marriage was a happy occasion, it meant saying good-bye to the Lloyds. James would become the minister at Deane and move into the parsonage, where the Lloyds were living. Before the Lloyds left for their new home in the village of Ibthorpe, seventeen miles away, Jane embroidered a needlework case for Mary and enclosed a note:

This little bag I hope will prove
To be not vainly made—
For, if you thread & needle want
It will afford you aid.

And as we are about to part
'Twill serve another end,
For when you look upon the bag
You'll recollect your friend.

For Jane, writing was the truest way to express herself, whether she was mocking a silly novel or saying farewell to a friend.

That year, Jane's cousin Jane Cooper became engaged to a naval commander. The Austens asked the Rev. Thomas Fowle, a former student of the Rev. Austen's school, to perform the wedding ceremony at Steventon Church. While preparing for the event, Tom fell in love with nineteen-year-old Cassandra. After a brief courtship with Jane, Tom became engaged to Cassandra instead. Like the Rev. Austen, Tom relied on a wealthy relation for his livelihood. He made a very modest living as a country parson. But his benefactor, Lord Craven, had promised Tom a better job, which would allow him to support a family. Tom and Cassandra decided to postpone their marriage until the new job was secured.

Jane Austen was also entering the world of courtship. Two months before her seventeenth birthday, she attended her first formal dance at Enham House, where her sister-in-law Elizabeth's family lived. She was accompanied by Cassandra and their friends Mary and Martha Lloyd. Before returning to Steventon, they went to a ball at Hurstbourne Park, the home of the Earl of Portsmouth and his family.

Jane had grown into an elegant young woman with sparkling hazel eyes and glowing pink cheeks. Her beautiful brown hair curled around her face. A family member remarked, "In person she was very attractive; her figure was rather tall and slender, her step light and firm." Jane's brother Henry remembered, "She was fond of dancing and excelled in it . . . . her carriage and deportment were quiet, yet graceful."

The Austens were frequently invited to private balls hosted by the local gentry (wealthy landowners). They also attended dances at the Basingstoke Assembly Rooms. Popular in the eighteenth century, assemblies were public balls open to those who paid a small fee to attend.

Dances, whether a formal ball or a last-minute family gathering, were important social events. Fashionable attire was essential, and women chose their clothes carefully. They paid close attention to many details, such as the trimming of a hat, the amount of lace on

Dances and parties were an important part of Jane's early adulthood.

a dress, and the color of a hair ribbon. Jane probably owned a good white muslin dress for dances and other special occasions.

Like all activities in Georgian England, attending a ball was ruled by strict etiquette. Single women had to have a chaperone, usually a male relative or an older married woman. Each man was expected to dance with many women throughout the evening so no one would feel left out. When not dancing, young people might chat as they lingered by the refreshment table or watched the other dancers.

Dancing was often done in groups. Men and women stood in lines opposite each other and danced the do-si-do or a type of square dance known in America as the Virginia reel. Partners stepped backward and forward, locking arms and twirling. The grander the dance, the more elaborate the music. An assembly room ball might include a small orchestra, while an impromptu dance at a neighbor's home usually featured an older single woman playing the piano.

The success of a ball depended on the quality and quantity of the guests. Days after a dance, women and men alike still gossiped about the guests—who was a poor dancer, who behaved badly, who was unfashionably dressed.

"THE INBETWEENITIES"

The balls gave Jane a rich supply of writing material, and she did not hesitate to cast a critical eye on the dancers. After one ball, she reported that she had met "two, broad featured" young ladies and "saw several fat girls with short noses." She described one guest as "a queer animal with a white neck" and commented on another's "two ugly naked shoulders!" After socializing with three sisters, she told Cassandra, "I was as civil to them as their bad breath would allow me."

Jane's stories reflected her sharp wit, but they showed a new maturity as well. In her unfinished story "Catharine, or The Bower," she began the shift from absurd, mocking storytelling to realistic portraits of country life. More and more she looked to her own life and family for inspiration. In one passage, she recalled Aunt Philadelphia's adventures in India.

In *Lady Susan,* a novel written as a series of letters, Jane created her first fully developed character. Lady Susan is a cruel woman who treats others horribly, even her own daughters. Jane may have based Lady Susan on Mrs. Craven, the Lloyd sisters' grandmother.

One of Jane's nieces later described the pieces that bridged the gap between her aunt's childhood stories and her adult writing as "inbetweenities, when the nonsense was passing away and before her wonderful talent had found it's [sic] proper channel."

Jane's pleasant routine of social visits, assembly balls, and writing was overshadowed by the dark cloud of war in 1793. In 1789 French peasants and laborers had risen up against the economic, political, and social oppression of the privileged classes. The French government was toppled, and a more democratic constitution was enacted. By 1793 the French Revolution entered its darkest period, known as the Reign of Terror. The French king, Louis XVI, was executed.

Other European nations, including Great Britain, feared that the fury in France would sweep across Europe and stir up their own working classes. In England, radicals were using the success of the French lower classes to call for revolution and reform. England and other countries stepped in to help the fallen French nobility. In February 1793, the leaders of the new French government declared war on England.

The Austens had two sons in the navy, Francis and Charles. They were joined in the fighting by Jane's favorite brother, Henry, who enlisted with the Oxfordshire militia. The Austens had hoped that Henry would become a minister, but he sought excitement and adventure. Jane wrote to her brothers regularly throughout the war. She continued to write to her two brothers in the navy as England and France fought various conflicts for the next twenty years.

"Every thing came finished from her pen; for on all subjects she had ideas as clear as her expressions were well chosen," Henry said. "She never dispatched a note or letter unworthy of publication."

This illustration shows the writing desk at which Jane composed her best-known works.

Chapter FIVE

DAYS OF SORROW

WHILE JANE HAD THE TALENT AND IMAGINATION TO be a writer, she did not have money to buy an equally important necessity—paper. Paper was an expensive luxury in the 1700s. But the Rev. Austen supplied drawing paper for Cassandra and writing paper for Jane. His generosity was more than a token of his love—he recognized the real promise of his daughters' talents. As further encouragement, he gave Jane a writing desk, which he bought in a Basingstoke store. The shopkeeper's records describe it as "a Small Mahogany Writing Desk with 1 Long Drawer and Glass Ink Stand."

The Rev. Austen was probably thinking about Jane's future as well. He knew that after his death, Steventon

Rectory would belong to the Church. If Jane was not married, she would have to rely on her brothers for a home. The Rev. Austen may have hoped that Jane could support herself, in part, by writing.

In her late teen years, Jane was pulled away from writing by family tragedies. In February 1794, Eliza's husband, the Comte de Feuillide, was guillotined (beheaded) in France. He was one of many victims of the Reign of Terror. Between 1793 and 1794, revolutionaries beheaded thousands of nobility and royalists.

Another blow came in May 1795 when James's wife, Anne, died suddenly at their home at Deane parsonage. James and his two-year-old daughter, Anna, were overwhelmed with grief. As a single father in a time when the care of children was mostly a woman's job, James turned to his mother and sisters for help. Anna spent the next two years at Steventon Rectory.

ELINOR AND MARIANNE

When Anna arrived at Steventon, nineteen-year-old Jane was writing her first full-length novel, called "Elinor and Marianne." The novel centers on two sisters. Marianne Dashwood is a romantic girl of seventeen. Although likeable, she is overly emotional and has unrealistic expectations of love and marriage. Elinor, the older sister, is Marianne's opposite—sensible, practical, and restrained. Like Jane and Cassandra, the Dashwood sisters are great readers and take pride in their literary knowledge.

Marianne is known for her "knack of finding her way in every house to the library." Her future husband, she tells her mother, must also enjoy reading. "He must enter into all my feelings: the same books, the same music must charm us both."

Elinor feels sorry for women who are not educated, such as her friend Lucy Steele. "Lucy was naturally clever... but she was ignorant and illiterate; and her deficiency of all mental improvement, her want of information in the most common particulars, could not be concealed."

While some critics believe that Jane modeled Marianne after herself and Elinor after Cassandra, the Austen family disagreed. "Cassandra had the *merit* of having her temper always under command, but Jane had the *happiness* of a temper that never required to be commanded," one family member wrote.

But "Elinor and Marianne" did reflect the economic realities of Jane and Cassandra's lives. After the death of Mr. Dashwood, Mrs. Dashwood and her daughters leave their home because their half-brother inherits it. By law, property passed from father to son. Fortunately, a distant relative invites the women to live in a modest cottage on his estate. The Dashwood sisters have reason to worry that they will not attract husbands because they have no dowry—money or property that a bride gives her husband when they are married.

Marianne especially feels the blow of her financial

circumstances. Her admirer Willoughby decides to marry a rich woman instead of Marianne. "My affection for Marianne . . . was insufficient to outweigh that dread of poverty," he explains.

As the daughter of a clergyman, Jane was painfully aware that her own options were limited. For most women, marriage was the only way to gain financial security, since they generally could not work to support themselves. Yet women without dowries—even if they came from good families or were beautiful and charming—had little chance of getting married. In the late 1700s, only thirty percent of women married.

For three years, Jane had watched as Cassandra waited for her fiancé's financial situation to improve. In October 1795, Tom Fowle's benefactor asked him to serve as clergy on a warship headed to the West Indies to stop a slave revolt. Lord Craven assured Tom that the long-awaited job as minister for a parish would be his as soon as the regiment returned to England. Tom saw the offer as a chance to secure the income he needed to marry Cassandra.

When Tom joined the regiment, his parents invited Cassandra to their home in Kintbury, about thirty miles from Steventon, for the Christmas holidays. For sisters as close as Jane and Cassandra, the separation was difficult. They knew, however, that they would face many such separations. In the eighteenth century, unmarried women were often called to the homes of friends and relations to assist with childbirth, to nurse sick children, to keep family members company, and to run households. Jane and Cassandra adapted to being apart by writing letters.

A GOOD-LOOKING YOUNG MAN

As Jane was finishing "Elinor and Marianne," she was attracting the attention of several suitors. She wrote to Cassandra on January 9, 1796, with a lively account of a dance she had attended at Manydown Park the night before. She giggled over young Charles Powlett, whose kiss she had refused, and described the rich Mr. Heartley, whose fortune did not tempt her.

One suitor did win Jane's approval. Tom Lefroy was the nephew of the Rev. Lefroy of Ashe Rectory. A recent graduate of Trinity College in Dublin, the young Irishman was in Ashe for a brief vacation before continuing his legal studies. Like Cassandra's Tom, Tom Lefroy relied on a wealthy relation for his livelihood.

Jane appeared to have fallen in love with Tom, whom she described as "very gentlemanlike, good-looking, [and] pleasant."

"I am almost afraid to tell you how my Irish friend and I behaved," Jane wrote to Cassandra after the Manydown ball. "Imagine to yourself everything most [shocking] in the way of dancing and sitting down together."

Later, Jane jokingly gave away her other suitors to Mary Lloyd: "Tell Mary that I make over Mr Heartley & all his Estate to her for her sole use and Benefit in

In his later years, Tom Lefroy admitted that he had once loved Jane Austen.

future, & not only him, but all my other Admirers into the bargain."

Jane thought that Tom might propose to her at an upcoming ball the Lefroys were hosting at Ashe Rectory. "I look forward with great impatience to it, as I rather expect to receive an offer from my friend in the course of the evening," she wrote to Cassandra the day before the dance. Giddy with expectation, she must have wished for her sister's company as she waited.

The next day, Jane had a different reason to long for Cassandra's companionship. The Rev. and Mrs. Lefroy, having realized the feelings between Jane and their nephew, forbade an engagement. They reminded Tom that marrying a poor clergyman's daughter would prevent him from advancing in society.

Brokenhearted, Jane would share one last dance with Tom. Before she left for Ashe Rectory, she wrote to Cassandra: "At length the Day is come on which I am to flirt my last with Tom Lefroy, & when you receive this it will be over—My tears flow as I write, at the melancholy idea."

First Impressions

Jane coped with her sadness over Tom Lefroy by beginning another novel, "First Impressions" (later *Pride and Prejudice*). In "First Impressions," Jane challenged the view that women were weak, inferior to men, and incapable of reason and judgment. Jane's characters, especially the heroine, Elizabeth Bennet, are very much like herself—they enjoy books and intelligent conversation. A hearty, healthy young woman, Elizabeth enjoys the outdoors and is confident in her own opinions.

When Elizabeth turns down a marriage proposal, her suitor persists, thinking she doesn't know her own mind. Elizabeth tells him, "Do not consider me now as an elegant female intending to plague you, but as a rational creature speaking the truth from her heart." Jane later wrote of Elizabeth, "I must confess that *I* think her as delightful a creature as ever appeared in print."

Even though Jane created female characters who

were strong and independent, she was not trying to abolish the social structure that shaped women's roles. Jane's books ended happily, with the heroines marrying men they loved. She only wanted to show what she knew to be true—that women were as capable and intelligent as men.

For example, when Jane Bennet becomes ill at a neighbor's house, Elizabeth wants to visit her sister. Since the family's carriage is not available, she walks the three miles in the rain. She arrives refreshed, and her visit cheers her sister. But others scold Elizabeth for walking in the rain and dirtying her skirts on the muddy path.

While Jane was writing "First Impressions," bad news arrived. In May 1797, the Austens learned that Tom Fowle, who was expected to return home from the West Indies that month, had died of a fever in February. The entire family felt the blow. Though devastated, Cassandra kept her feelings to herself, much like Elinor concealed her emotions in "Elinor and Marianne." In his will, Tom left Cassandra one thousand pounds.

Jane and Cassandra had each loved and lost, and the sisters grew even closer. "[They] were everything to each other," their niece Anna remembered in later years. "They seemed to lead a life to themselves within the general family life."

A sad year for Cassandra brought happiness for James, who married Mary Lloyd. James, Mary, and

Anna settled back into the rectory at Deane. Henry surprised his family by marrying their dazzling cousin Eliza in December. Among the middle and upper classes, it was not unusual for first cousins to marry. The Austens, however, had not realized that Henry was in love with Eliza.

Jane finished "First Impressions" in August 1797, when she was twenty-one. Her family liked the novel so much that her father decided it should be published. He wrote to Thomas Cadell, a London publisher, and asked if he could send the manuscript for consideration. He did not describe the story but only compared its length to *Evelina,* a popular novel by Fanny Burney. Mr. Cadell sent a brief response, "Declined by return of Post."

The rejection must have been a disappointment, and Jane was already troubled by the many sorrows that had fallen on her family. When Jane learned that her cousin Philadelphia had lost her father, she wrote, "I will not press you to write . . . but when you can do it without pain I hope we shall receive from you . . . an account of my Aunt & Yourself . . . in these early days of Sorrow."

Cassandra drew this watercolor sketch of Jane. It is believed to be one of the only original images of Jane that exists.

Chapter SIX

EXPERIMENTAL HOUSEKEEPING

JANE'S DAYS OF SORROW WERE FOLLOWED IN THE summer of 1798 by a family visit to Edward's home in Kent. Jane, Cassandra, and their parents enjoyed the leisurely life at Godmersham. The Knights—the adoptive parents of Edward Austen—like others in the upper class, had inherited their land and wealth. They lived in beautifully decorated homes and wore fine clothes made by tailors. Governesses and tutors looked after the children. While the Austens had a few servants, the family members still helped with household chores. At Godmersham, dozens of servants saw to the comfort of the Knight family and their guests. Life was a steady stream of visits, parties, new clothes, and pretty things. Men enjoyed hunting, traveling, and politics. Women occupied themselves with music, fancy needlework, and social visits. Jane once declared, "Kent is the only place for happiness, Everybody is rich there."

Jane especially appreciated the estate's vast library, where she wrote in comfort and style. She revised "Elinor and Marianne" into a novel she called *Sense and Sensibility*. In October Edward's wife, Elizabeth, gave birth to a son. Elizabeth disapproved of Jane's novel writing and sharp wit. She asked Cassandra—

Edward inherited Godmersham in Kent, England, after the death of his wealthy adoptive parents. The Austen family originally came from Kent.

and not Jane—to remain at Godmersham to help with the child.

At the end of the month, Jane and her parents returned to Steventon. Mrs. Austen arrived home ill and spent the next five weeks in bed. With Cassandra away, it was Jane's duty to act as lady of the house while her mother recovered. In addition to nursing Mrs. Austen, Jane planned meals, kept her father company in the evening, received visitors, and kept up the family's regular correspondence.

At first, Jane assumed these duties with her usual sunny nature. She enjoyed trying new dishes, including plump dumplings and ox-cheek.

"I am very fond of experimental housekeeping," she wrote to Cassandra. "I always take care to provide such things as please my own appetite, which I consider as the chief merit in housekeeping. My mother desires me to tell you that I am a very good housekeeper."

A HOUSE DERANGED

Jane's happy housekeeping was short-lived. Problems soon arose with the servants. The family's maid, Mrs. Hilliard, became ill, and the washerwoman quit. "Our family affairs are rather deranged at present," Jane informed Cassandra. The remaining maid needed to be replaced, because, Jane observed, "she does not look as if anything she touched would ever be clean."

Between running the house, hiring new servants,

and nursing Mrs. Austen, Jane was also hurrying back and forth to Deane Rectory. There, her sister-in-law and friend Mary Lloyd Austen was expecting her first child. The winter of 1798 was cold and rainy, and the usually pleasant Deane Lane was covered with mud.

The bleak weather spilled over into Jane's spirits and darkened her usually cheerful mood. It seemed as if everyone irritated her. Her brother James annoyed her by helping himself to Cassandra's dwindling supply of drawing paper. A visit from her dear friend Anne Lefroy only brought bittersweet memories of her brief romance with Anne's nephew Tom Lefroy. Mary safely had a son on November 17, but spending time with the baby strained Jane's nerves.

Elbow deep in illness and housekeeping, Jane was also jealous of Cassandra, who was enjoying the comforts of Godmersham. While Jane slogged through the mud on Deane Lane, she imagined Cassandra strolling around the parklike grounds of Godmersham or reading a novel in the library. Cassandra had even attended a dance where the Prince of Wales was a guest.

Cassandra's letters were one of Jane's few pleasures, yet she even bristled with her sister. She chided Cassandra for her slow replies. In one letter, she hinted that Cassandra was too busy to read her letters all the way through. When Cassandra wrote that she hoped to read "First Impressions" again, Jane replied, "I do not wonder at your wanting to read 'First Impressions' again, so seldom as you have gone through it."

LETTER WRITING

n the late 1700s, improvements in mail service helped make letter writing fashionable among the middle and upper classes throughout Great Britain. The Austen siblings often walked from Steventon Rectory to the gate at the end of Deane Lane to collect the family's letters.

In the centuries before the invention of the telegraph and telephone made communication instantaneous, writing letters was one of the few ways friends and family could exchange information. Letters announced births and deaths, conveyed other family news, and kept up social ties. The task of writing to relatives often fell to women.

Women also wrote letters to maintain friendships, for intellectual stimulation, and as a pleasurable pastime. Still, the rules of society extended to letter writing. Single women could write only to other women and close male relatives. Correspondence between an unmarried man and woman was a sign that they were engaged. In Jane's novels, some of her characters broke this rule, and Jane herself wrote to her male publishers.

Just as composing clever letters was considered a skill, handwriting was almost an art form. Jane always thought her penmanship was inferior to Cassandra's. "I am quite angry with myself for not writing closer," she wrote to her sister. "Why is my alphabet so much more sprawly than Yours?"

However much she disliked her handwriting, Jane considered herself a good correspondent. During her lifetime, she wrote hundreds, perhaps thousands, of letters, although only about 150 survive. "I have now attained the true art of letter-writing," Jane wrote to Cassandra in 1801, "which...is to express on paper exactly what one would say to the same person by word of mouth."

The local balls were also losing their appeal. In an effort to economize, the Rev. Austen had given up the family's carriage. Twenty-three-year-old Jane had to rely on her brothers or neighbors for a ride to the dances. This year, suitors did not rush to her side to request a dance. She lamented to her sister after one ball, "I do not think I was very much in request. People were rather apt not to ask me [to dance] till they could not help it; One's Consequence you know varies so much at times without any particular reason."

Jane had little time that winter for writing. No doubt this was on her mind when the Rev. Austen bought a copy of Egerton Brydges's newest book, *Arthur Fitz-Albini: A Novel.* Even though he was a family acquaintance, Jane was no fan of the pompous writer. She wrote hotly to Cassandra, "There is very little story, and what there is [is] told in a strange, unconnected way. My father is disappointed—*I* am not, for I expected nothing better."

Jane looked forward to January, when a new library in Basingstoke would begin circulating books. Subscribers paid a fee to borrow books, and most libraries allowed each subscriber to borrow two or three books at a time.

Toward the end of December, Mrs. Austen was feeling better. Although she had been legitimately ill, she often exaggerated her symptoms and was a difficult patient. Jane had grown tired of her mother's dramatic behavior.

Jane's gloomy mood faded away when she spent time outdoors. In nature she found solitude and relief from family responsibilities. One frigid day, with a thick, icy frost covering the Steventon countryside, Jane bundled up and walked alone to Deane. Despite the bad weather, her spirits lifted a little with each cautious step across the slippery country lane. "I do not know that I ever did such a thing in my life before," Jane wrote triumphantly to Cassandra.

As her mood began to brighten, Jane was somewhat ashamed of her complaining letters. She instructed Cassandra, "Seize upon the Scissors as soon as you possibly can on the receipt of this."

A CHANGE OF SCENE

Jane stepped into the new year with "a cold & weakness in one of [her] eyes." The condition made it difficult to write to Cassandra or work on her new novel, *Susan*. Nevertheless, she had something to look forward to. In March, Cassandra returned and Jane gladly turned over the household management to her. In May, Edward Austen invited Jane and Mrs. Austen to join him in the city of Bath to enjoy the therapeutic waters of the spa there.

Jane was especially excited to go to Bath because it gave her the perfect opportunity to work on *Susan*, which she set in Bath. *Susan* tells the story of Catherine Morland, a girl who reads too many Gothic novels. Gothic tales, all the rage in the 1790s, were dark, brooding stories of the supernatural. Popular Gothic novels included *The Mysteries of Udolpho* by Ann Radcliffe and *The Monk* by Matthew Lewis.

In Jane's novel, Catherine is invited to stay at Northanger Abbey, the home of the Tilney family. Catherine is in love with Henry Tilney. Although he teasingly feeds her obsession with Gothic horror, Henry shares Catherine's fondness for novels. He tells her, "The person, be it gentleman or lady, who has not pleasure in a good novel, must be intolerably stupid."

On Catherine's first visit to the Tilney home, a torrential rainstorm pelts down on Northanger Abbey. She works herself into a full-blown Gothic frenzy when she spots an old chest of drawers tucked away in her guest room. Late at night, with the wind howling, Catherine searches the chest and finds a "manuscript." But the wind blows out her candle and she must wait until the next morning to read it.

"Her greedy eyes glanced rapidly over a page. . . . Could it be possible, or did not her senses play her false? She held a washingbill in hand. Such was the collection of papers which had filled her with expectation and alarm, and robbed her of half her night's rest!"

In another frenzy, Catherine convinces herself that Henry's father is keeping his wife prisoner, locked up in Northanger Abbey. Despite her foolishness, Henry asks Catherine to marry him, and she accepts.

In Bath, Jane was also thinking about "First Impressions," the subject of the query letter her father had sent to a London publisher two years earlier. The story of the Bennet sisters was still a family favorite, read again and again. Jane often carried her manuscripts with her when she traveled. While Jane was in Bath, Cassandra wrote to tell her that Martha Lloyd had asked to reread "First Impressions."

Jane jokingly replied, "I would not let Martha read 'First Impressions' again upon any account, & am very glad that I did not leave it in your power.—She is very cunning, but I see through her design;—she means to publish it from Memory, & one more perusal [will] enable her to do it."

Named for the region's hot springs, the city of Bath traces its origins to the ancient Romans. In the 1700s, Bath flourished as a fashionable resort for the upper class, who were drawn to the city's spas, above.

Chapter SEVEN

BATH

THE FIRST YEAR OF A NEW CENTURY BROUGHT LITTLE
change to Jane's steady life. Back home in Steventon
at the end of the summer, she wrote regularly and attended local dances. And she helped her parents make
elaborate changes to the rectory garden.

"Our Improvements have advanced very well," she
told Cassandra in the fall of 1800. "[T]he Bank along
the *Elm Walk* is sloped down for the reception of
Thorns & Lilacs; & it is settled that the other side of
the path is to continue turf'd & be planted with
Beech, Ash, & Larch."

In November, the Austens lost several trees in a
storm, including Jane's favorite "highly valued Elms."
Around the same time, Cassandra was with Edward at

Godmersham, and Jane enjoyed a relaxing visit with the Lloyds in Ibthorpe. She and Martha returned to Steventon in early December. The Rev. Austen greeted them with a shocking announcement: "Well, girls, it is all settled, we have decided to leave Steventon . . . and go to Bath." While Jane was away, the Rev. Austen had decided to retire.

Unaware that her parents were even considering a move, Jane was shocked by the news. According to a family story, she fainted when she learned she would be leaving the only home she had known.

Whatever her reaction, by January 1801, Jane and her parents were busy with plans for packing, moving, and finding a home in Bath. "[T]here is something interesting in the bustle of going away," she wrote to Cassandra.

Moving a household was expensive. The Rev. Austen decided to sell most of the Steventon furniture and buy new things in Bath. He hired an auctioneer, and neighboring families bought many of the Austens' belongings, including the chickens and Jane's piano.

The Rev. Austen transferred his parish to his son James. James prepared to move into Steventon Rectory with his daughter, Anna, now seven, his wife, Mary, and their two-year-old son, James Edward.

Mrs. Austen and Jane traveled to Bath in May. While they looked for a house to rent, they stayed with Mrs. Austen's brother, James Leigh-Perrot, and his wife, Jane. Cassandra and the Rev. Austen would join them in June.

Jane Austen sent details about the latest fashions in Bath to her sister. "Black gauze Cloaks are worn as much as anything," she wrote. She was pleased that her straw bonnet was just as nice as the ones worn by ladies in Bath.

Soon, however, the novelty of new surroundings wore off. Jane was bored with the company of older people and husband-hunting single women. "Another stupid party last night," Jane wrote. "I cannot anyhow continue to find people agreeable."

"THE SUBJECT OF HOUSES"

Jane's first weeks in Bath were also troubled by money worries. Comfortable yet affordable housing was almost impossible to find. Jane looked at several places, but one house was "not inviting," another had "monstrously little" rooms, and others were either damp or too small. After three weeks, she had had enough. "I have nothing more to say on the subject of Houses," she wrote to Cassandra.

Finally, the *Bath Chronicle* newspaper advertised a house overlooking the Sydney Gardens, a public park. The Austens found the house affordable and suitable. Jane was pleased to be near the park, which was beautifully landscaped with waterfalls and a labyrinthine (mazelike) hedge. While the landlord readied the house, the Austens traveled to the seashore in the county of Devon in western England. Jane enjoyed "sea bathing" and walks along the coast.

While Jane was on vacation in Devon, she met a pleasant, handsome young clergyman. Jane, twenty-five years old, was lively and attractive, and the two began falling in love. When the Austens prepared to travel farther along the coast to another town, the young man asked Jane if he could see her again. She agreed. Excited, Jane confided to Cassandra about her new romance. But when the time came to meet, the clergyman was not there. Instead, Jane received a letter announcing his death.

The years following the move from Steventon were difficult for Jane. The Austens lived a transitory life. They moved in and out of a series of rented homes in Bath. They took long holidays and stayed for extended visits with relatives and friends at Steventon, Kent, and Southampton. For Jane, the upheaval was devastating. It was hard to write novels while traveling.

A Proposal

In December 1802, Jane and Cassandra traveled to Manydown Park to visit their old friends the Bigg family. Just six miles from Steventon, the grand house held many happy memories for Jane. She and the Bigg sisters had enjoyed walks around the estate, and after Basingstoke balls they had gossiped late into the night. And it was at Manydown that Jane had fallen in love with Tom Lefroy.

One Friday evening shortly after her arrival, Jane was taken off guard when the Biggs' younger brother,

Harris, asked her to marry him. Jane was weary from her travels. Back among friends, enjoying the luxury of a fine home, she agreed to become Harris's wife.

Almost immediately, Jane realized that she had made a mistake. She knew the marriage would provide financial security. She longed for a comfortable life and a home of her own. But she did not love Harris. That night, she and Cassandra struggled with Jane's predicament. It wasn't unusual for women to marry out of a sense of family duty or to ensure their fortune. Cousin Eliza, whom Jane loved and respected, had done so when she married the French count. But Jane believed in passionate love. "I consider everybody as having a right to marry *once* in their Lives for Love," she once wrote. Jane chose not to betray her ideals. She could not marry a man she did not love. The next morning, Jane explained her decision to Harris, and she and Cassandra left Manydown.

The sisters fled to Steventon. They begged James to take them to Bath that day. Jane and Cassandra had to rely on their father and brothers for transportation, since it was considered improper for single women to travel alone by public coach. The trip must have been a quiet one—Cassandra and Jane refused to explain themselves.

Before long, news of Jane's brief engagement spread through the Steventon neighborhood. While some members of her family disapproved of her decision, others admired her. One of Jane's nieces later wrote,

"I have always respected her for her courage. I believe most young women . . . would have gone on trusting to love after marriage."

Back in Bath, Jane buried herself in her writing. The incident at Manydown may have inspired her to begin *The Watsons,* a novel about four sisters. The story involves the Watson sisters' attempts to find husbands before their father, an elderly clergyman, dies. The sisters' circumstances were very much like her own. Jane never finished the novel. She turned back to her earlier work, *Susan,* revising it and making a copy by hand. To her delight, her brother Henry offered to see about having it published. He had founded a financial firm in London a few years earlier and had connections in the publishing business.

This time, Jane received good news. In the spring of 1803, publisher Richard Crosby purchased the copyright to *Susan* for ten pounds. He promised that the book would be published soon.

PAINFUL LOSSES

Once again, life's difficulties overshadowed Jane's writing. With continuing money problems, the Austens moved to less expensive housing in October 1804. In late December, Jane learned that she had lost a dear friend. Anne Lefroy had died in a riding accident on Jane's twenty-ninth birthday.

More sadness quickly followed. After a short illness, the Rev. Austen died at home in Bath on January 21,

1805. Jane wrote to her brothers with the news: "Our dear Father has closed his virtuous & happy life, in a death almost as free from suffering as his Children could have wished."

Sad and alone, the Austen women were also practically penniless. With the Rev. Austen's death, they had to depend on the goodwill of their other male relations. Mrs. Austen and Cassandra had invested small sums of money that paid them a modest annual income, but it was not enough to live on. Jane had nothing. Later, Edward's adoptive mother, Catherine Knight, who had always liked Jane, began giving her a regular allowance.

After the Rev. Austen's death, the Austen women moved again to save money. Their situation was almost identical to that of the Dashwood women in *Sense and Sensibility*.

In April, Jane's good friend Martha Lloyd also lost a parent when her mother died at their home in Ibthorpe. Like Mrs. Austen and her daughters, Martha now relied on the generosity of family and friends. The Austens invited her to live with them. By pooling their meager resources, the Austens and Martha Lloyd improved their situations.

Now a foursome of women, the Austen household picked up and traveled again. They stayed with James and Mary at Steventon, with Francis and his new wife, Mary, in Southampton, and with Edward and Elizabeth at Godmersham. Despite the upheaval of

Martha Lloyd, left, and Jane had much in common. Martha also was a clergyman's daughter and her mother had ties to a prestigious family. When Martha was in her sixties, she married Jane's brother Francis Austen.

travel, Jane enjoyed visiting her brothers and their growing families. Edward and Elizabeth's home at Godmersham was an especially enjoyable retreat. In the summer of 1808, Jane spent a few weeks there. Then it was Cassandra's turn to stay there to help with the birth of Elizabeth's eleventh child.

Soon after the baby boy was born, Elizabeth died. Cassandra remained at Godmersham to help. In the meantime, Jane arranged to have two of Edward's sons, thirteen-year-old George and fourteen-year-old Edward, join her in Southampton. When the grieving boys arrived, Jane gave them her full attention. The trio played games, made up riddles, and floated paper boats on the river. One day Jane took them on a ferry ride to view the construction of a navy warship, and another day they enjoyed a rowboat ride.

Not long after his wife's death, Edward offered his

mother and sisters something they hadn't had since they left Steventon nine years earlier—a permanent home. Edward had recently inherited more Knight property, and he gave the Austens the choice of two homes. The women chose a house in Chawton, a town in their native Hampshire. The location was also convenient for family members to visit. Edward promised to bring his family often. Francis and Charles would come when they were on leave from naval duty, and Henry's bank had a branch office in nearby Alton. Chawton was only seventeen miles from Steventon, so James and his family could also visit.

As Jane prepared to move to her new home, she attended to business. In 1809, six years after Henry had sold the copyright to *Susan,* Jane wrote to the publisher. She told Mr. Crosby that unless she heard from him, she would send *Susan* to another publisher. Wanting to conceal her identity, Jane used the alias Mrs. Ashton Dennis, which allowed her to sign her letter "MAD."

Crosby's reply made her even madder. "The [manuscript] shall be yours for the same as we paid for it," he told her.

Jane could not afford to buy back her manuscript. After she purchased necessities such as laundry services and postage and bought small gifts for her family, what little money remained had to be saved.

"Single Women have a dreadful propensity for being poor," she wrote years later.

Jane wrote several novels while living at Chawton Cottage. The home is now a Jane Austen museum.

Chapter EIGHT

CHAWTON

EVEN THOUGH **R**ICHARD **C**ROSBY WAS NOT GOING TO publish *Susan,* Jane was content with her life. She wrote chatty notes full of plans for the house in Chawton. She hoped the property had a garden and pretty grounds. She was pleased that "[e]very body is acquainted with Chawton & speaks of it as a remarkably pretty village."

In the spring of 1809, Edward arranged for repairs to be made to Chawton Cottage. Soon after moving in, Jane wrote to Francis:

> Our Chawton home, how much we find
> Already in it, to our mind;
> And how convinced, that when complete

It will all other Houses beat,
That ever have been made or mended,
With rooms concise, or rooms distended.
You'll find us very snug next year.

Built in the late 1600s, the "cottage" was a sturdy red brick house with six bedrooms. Its low, roughly finished ceilings were much like those in Steventon Rectory. A washhouse, bakehouse, and outhouse stood in the backyard. The property even included a small pond.

Once an inn or tavern, Chawton Cottage overlooked

Chawton's church, natural beauty, and residents all added to its rural charm. Jane said she was happy living there.

the intersection of two busy roads. Edward had one front window bricked up and a bookcase built in its place. Another window was added on the side of the house, overlooking trees and grass. Behind the house, hedges bordered walking paths. The Austens planted an orchard and garden that produced strawberries, apricots, peas, gooseberries, potatoes, and many other fruits and vegetables. Although Jane's new home was nothing like Godmersham, Manydown, or other grand houses, Jane was comfortable and happy there.

Like Steventon, Chawton was a rural village, and most of the villagers worked as farm laborers. The Austens became friendly with some families in the neighborhood, but they did not establish close ties.

AUNT JANE

By 1810 Jane and Cassandra had eighteen nieces and nephews. James's children—Anna, James Edward, and Caroline—visited Chawton often. Jane looked forward to their visits. "I have always maintained the importance of Aunts," she once wrote.

Caroline enjoyed her playful, loving aunt. "Everything she could make amusing to a child," she later said. "She would tell us the most delightful stories chiefly of Fairyland, and her Fairies had all characters of their own . . . . She was the one we always looked to for help—She would furnish us with what we wanted from her wardrobe, and she would often be the entertaining visitor in our make believe house."

NOVELISTS IN JANE'S ERA

During Jane Austen's lifetime, the novel was still a relatively new form of writing. A long work of fiction written in prose, the novel grew out of earlier writing forms, including verse and short stories.

The first English-language novel was Daniel Defoe's *Robinson Crusoe,* published in 1719. By the end of the 1700s, more and more novels were being written and published. The growing middle class read novels as a pastime, and the rise of circulating libraries gave readers access to more books.

The number of women who were writing and publishing also began to increase shortly before Jane was born. One of the best-known female writers of the time was Fanny Burney, the author of *Evelina* and other novels. Jane admired Burney. In fact, she later borrowed the phrase "pride and prejudice" for one of her own novels from Burney's *Cecilia.*

Although readers enjoyed novels, some critics said they were frivolous and immoral. Women were expected to read only books that offered moral instruction and helped them improve their character and household skills.

Female novelists were less likely to be made fun of if their books showed women in traditional roles. Some female writers encouraged women to follow men's wishes. They promoted this message not only in novels but also in etiquette books known as "conduct" books.

Other writers supported women's rights. They were criticized for their views, however. While Jane shared many of these feminist beliefs, her feminism was subtle. To convey the idea that marriage should be a partnership based on mutual respect, for example, she created characters whose marriages met this ideal.

Life at Chawton Cottage provided a steady routine for Jane. Mrs. Austen, now in her seventies, relied on the younger women to run the household. In the early mornings, Jane practiced piano, then made breakfast for the household. Once the meal was cleared away, she was free for the rest of the day. Often she spent much of the day in the dining room, writing at a small round table. Sometimes she moved to the drawing room and wrote at the mahogany desk her father had given her.

Jane was careful to conceal what she was doing. "She wrote upon small sheets of paper which could easily be put away, or covered with a piece of blotting paper," her nephew James Edward remembered.

Although Jane's immediate family knew about her writing, she hid her literary activities from neighbors, friends, and servants. During Jane's lifetime, writing for publication and money was not considered respectable for women, even though more and more people were buying and reading novels.

A creaking door to the dining room helped keep Jane's secret. "She objected to having the little inconvenience remedied, because it gave her notice when anyone was coming," her nephew James Edward wrote.

Almost immediately after moving to Chawton in July 1809, Jane picked up her pen. Beginning with a revision of *Sense and Sensibility,* the stories flowed out, unstoppable.

SENSE

AND

SENSIBILITY:

A NOVEL.

IN THREE VOLUMES.

BY A LADY.

VOL. I.

Wanting to keep her authorship a secret, Jane identified herself only as "a lady" when she published her first novel, Sense and Sensibility.

Chapter NINE

SUCCESS

WHEN JANE TOLD HER FAMILY SHE WAS WRITING again, they all supported her. They had always enjoyed her stories, particularly "First Impressions." During the years between Steventon and Chawton, Jane often read aloud from her work. She was a good storyteller. "Her voice was extremely sweet," her brother Henry said. "She delivered herself with fluency and precision."

Henry was especially interested in his sister's writing. He encouraged Jane to submit another book for publication. She suggested that Henry act as her literary agent for *Sense and Sensibility*. He contacted Thomas Egerton, a London publisher. Egerton agreed to publish Jane's novel if she would sign a contract promising to reimburse him if her book lost money. Considering her bad experience with Richard Crosby, Jane made a bold move by agreeing to Egerton's terms. She was so certain that her novel would lose money, however, that she set aside money from her small allowance to pay for the losses.

By the end of March 1811, Jane was in London correcting the page proofs for *Sense and Sensibility*. The proofs—typeset pages from the printer—were her last chance to correct mistakes before the book was printed. In London, Jane stayed with Henry and Eliza. They took her to the theater, concerts, and art galleries and included her in the parties they hosted. Despite her active social life, Jane was preoccupied with her book. "I am never too busy to think of S&S," she told Cassandra. "I can no more forget it, than a mother can forget her suckling child."

Only a small circle of close relatives and friends knew that Jane was about to publish her first book. While Jane was in London, Cassandra wrote to their relations and asked them to keep Jane's identity a secret. Cassandra was worried about Jane's reputation.

AN "ENTERTAINING NARRATIVE"

As it happened, Cassandra's worries were unnecessary. *Sense and Sensibility* was first advertised at the end of October 1811 in two London newspapers, *The Star* and *The Morning Chronicle*. The book's author was identified only as "a lady."

At last, Jane's writing reached a wide audience. *Sense and Sensibility* was praised as "well written, highly pleasing, interesting" and an "entertaining narrative." One reviewer credited the author with "much knowledge of character" and "a good deal of sense."

Encouraged, Jane worked on revising "First Impressions" throughout 1812. When she was finished, she renamed the novel *Pride and Prejudice*. In November, Henry sold *Pride and Prejudice* to Egerton for 100 pounds. This time Jane was not at risk financially. *Pride and Prejudice* was published at the end of January 1813.

Just as Jane's writing was often interrupted by family responsibilities, her success was also not entirely her own. She had to rely on Henry to handle transactions with the publisher. When *Pride and Prejudice* arrived at Chawton, Jane wrote triumphantly to Cassandra, "I have got my own darling Child from London." But instead of the three copies she had asked for, Henry sent only one. He gave her other copies to Edward and Charles. "I wrote to [Henry] immediately to beg for my two other Sets, however he was gone before my Letter was written . . . . [N]othing more can be done till his return," Jane told Cassandra.

Rather than fuming about Henry's forgetfulness, Jane decided to enjoy her secret authorship. The day *Pride and Prejudice* arrived, the Austens were entertaining a neighbor, Miss Benn. After dinner, Jane read

This illustration is from an edition of Pride and Prejudice *published in 1833. It shows Elizabeth Bennet talking intently with Bingley about Mr. Darcy and Lydia.*

aloud from the book without revealing the author. "I beleive [sic] it passed with her unsuspected," Jane wrote to Cassandra. She was pleased that Miss Benn "really does seem to admire Elizabeth."

More good news followed the publication of *Pride and Prejudice*. "You will be glad to hear that every Copy of S.&S. is sold & that it has brought me £140— besides the Copyright," Jane wrote to Francis in July 1813. "I have now therefore written myself into £250.—which only makes me long for more."

A SECRET REVEALED

With 750 copies of *Sense and Sensibility* sold, Jane was no longer a poor spinster but a successful novelist. She did not have to pinch and save. She could enjoy her wealth—two hundred and fifty pounds was more than enough money to live on for a year. While visiting Henry in London, Jane bought dress material for Cassandra. Knowing that Cassandra would not approve of such extravagance, Jane warned her, "It will be a great pleasure to me. Don't say a word."

At first, *Pride and Prejudice* received little attention from reviewers. But by May 1813, it was considered *the* fashionable novel in England. A review in the *British Critic* praised the character Elizabeth Bennet as "superior... to the common heroines of novels."

Within a few months, Henry, bursting with pride, was revealing his sister's secret identity to almost anyone who would listen. Soon Henry's rich and influential friends wanted to meet the author of *Pride and Prejudice* and *Sense and Sensibility*. Although flattered by Henry's admiration, Jane was annoyed that he ignored her wishes to remain anonymous.

In the summer of 1813, Edward brought his family to stay at Chawton Cottage while Godmersham was being repainted. Their presence cheered Jane, who was saddened by the death of her cousin Eliza, Henry's wife, earlier that year. In September, Jane returned to Godmersham with Edward's family, staying until November. In the estate's large library, she worked on a novel called *Mansfield Park*. She no longer tried to keep her writing a secret. Her niece Marianne Knight remembered that while at Godmersham, "Aunt Jane would sit quietly... beside the fire in the library, saying nothing for a good while, and then would suddenly burst out laughing, jump up and run across the room to a table where pens and paper were lying, write something down, and then come back to the fire."

Jane was consumed by writing. As she prepared to return to Chawton, she wrote to Cassandra, "I wonder whether the Ink bottle has been filled."

When Jane's nieces and nephews learned that their aunt was the author of the latest best-sellers, they flocked to Chawton with literary ambitions of their own. Fourteen-year-old James Edward wrote a verse for Jane:

> No words can express, my dear Aunt, my surprise
> Or make you conceive how I opened my eyes,
> Like a pig Butcher Pile has just struck with
>   his knife,

When I heard for the very first time in my life
That I had the honour to have a relation
Whose Works were dispersed through the whole
   of the nation.

MANSFIELD PARK

Six months after Eliza's death, Henry again acted as
Jane's agent, negotiating a contract with Egerton to
publish *Mansfield Park*. In May 1814, the novel was
published in three volumes. Jane, who was now thirty-
eight, identified herself only as "the author of *Pride
and Prejudice* and *Sense and Sensibility*." Unlike the
first two books Jane published, *Mansfield Park* was
not a revision of something she had written in her
early twenties.

   The heroine of *Mansfield Park*, Fanny Price, is a
plain, shy, poor girl who is taken in by a rich uncle
and his family on their estate, Mansfield Park. Fanny
is so meek and timid that her pompous cousins either
ignore her or treat her unkindly. "Few young ladies of
eighteen could be less called on to speak their opinion
than Fanny," Jane wrote in *Mansfield Park*. Only
cousin Edmund pays any attention to Fanny and
helps her build her confidence. Fanny falls in love
with Edmund. After first falling for the shallow Mary
Crawford, Edmund finally recognizes Fanny's quiet affection and falls in love with her.

   As *Mansfield Park* was being published, Jane began
her fourth novel, *Emma*. Meanwhile, reading and

writing were becoming popular pastimes in Chawton. Neighbors exchanged books with a flurry and even made plans to begin a literary club. "We are quite run over with Books," Jane told Cassandra.

A FAMILY OF WRITERS

Jane's niece Caroline, just eleven, jotted down verses and short stories for her aunt to read. Jane always replied with encouraging letters. Years later, Caroline wrote, "I am sorry to think how I troubled her with reading them. She was very kind about it, and always had some praise to bestow."

Teenage James Edward was also writing a novel. He was thrilled when Jane described it as "extremely clever; written with great ease & spirit;—if he can carry it on in the same way, it will be a firstrate work."

Some of Jane's first works were dedicated to her niece Anna, right, *after whom Jane is said to have modeled her character Emma.*

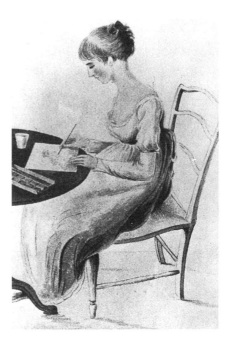

Cassandra drew this picture of her niece Fanny Knight in the early 1800s.

While Jane loved all her nieces and nephews, she especially enjoyed Fanny and Anna, her older nieces. Anna shared her aunt's sparkling wit. At twenty-one, Anna was about the same age Jane had been when she wrote *Sense and Sensibility*. Jane took time out from working on *Emma* to read Anna's manuscript, "Which Is the Heroine?" Jane advised Anna to write about the people and places she knew best. She wrote to Anna, "You are now collecting your People delightfully, getting them exactly into such a spot as is the delight of my life;—3 or 4 Families in a Country Village is the very thing to work on."

In this illustration from Emma, the heroine paints Harriet's picture while Mr. Elton looks on.

Chapter **TEN**

"MY OWN STYLE"

AT AGE THIRTY-EIGHT, JANE AUSTEN HAD PUBLISHED
three successful books and was creating a heroine
"whom no one but myself will much like." Emma
Woodhouse would be Jane's most spirited heroine.
Jane's niece Anna, a difficult but lovable young
woman, may have inspired the character of Emma.

In the novel, Emma Woodhouse—"handsome, clever,
and rich"—convinces herself that she has successfully
paired her former governess with a local widower.
When she takes credit for the marriage, a family
friend, Mr. Knightley, warns her against matchmaking:
"You made a lucky guess; and that is all that can be
said." Nevertheless, Emma moves from one disastrous
matchmaking attempt to another.

While she is quick to pair off others, Emma herself is not anxious to marry. She believes that women should marry for love. "If a woman doubts as to whether she should accept a man or not, she certainly ought to refuse him," Emma tells a friend. "If she can hesitate as to 'Yes,' she ought to say 'No,' directly."

With Mr. Knightley's help, Emma finally understands that her meddling is doing more harm than good. Soon she realizes her true feelings for her old friend, and the two are married.

While writing *Mansfield Park,* Jane had worried that it wouldn't be as popular as *Pride and Prejudice.* Now she worried about *Emma.* "I am strongly haunted with the idea that to those readers who have preferred *Pride and Prejudice* it will appear inferior in wit," she said.

As Jane was working on *Emma, Mansfield Park* sold out its first printing. Jane earned about three hundred and fifty pounds. She traveled to London in November to arrange for a second edition. Egerton refused, without giving a reason—though *Mansfield Park* lacked the sparkle of Jane's previous novels. Jane was also disappointed that the book had not been reviewed. Frustrated, she asked family members and friends for their comments and collected them into *Opinions of Mansfield Park.* For the most part, Jane's friends and family reinforced what they had told her all along—*Pride and Prejudice* was still the favorite. While Fanny Knight loved Fanny Price, Anna Austen Lefroy "could not bear" her and Mrs. Austen called the character "insipid."

A Book for a Prince

Jane sold *Emma* to another London publisher, John
Murray, in September 1815. Shortly after Murray
agreed to publish *Emma*, Henry became gravely ill.
Jane stayed with him as he recovered. While he was
ill, several doctors were called to his side, including a
personal physician to the Prince of Wales, heir to the
throne of England. This doctor confided to Jane that
the prince admired her novels. Soon, Jane was contacted by the prince's librarian, James Stanier Clarke.
Clarke invited her to visit the prince's library at Carl-
ton House, his London residence. While she was
there, Clarke suggested that Jane could dedicate her
next book to the prince. *Emma* was published in three

*Jane gave these red
leather-bound copies
of* Emma *to the Prince
of Wales in 1815.*

volumes in December 1815 and was "Dedicated by Permission to H.R.H. The Prince Regent." Before the book was released to the public, she sent an edition of the volumes, bound in red leather, to the prince.

Jane was a little irritated that the prince did not thank her personally for the copy of *Emma* she sent to him, or for the dedication. When Clarke suggested that her next project should be a historical romance dedicated to the prince's future son-in-law, an amused Jane refused. "I could no more write a Romance than an Epic Poem," she wrote to Clarke. "I am sure I should be hung before I had finished the first Chapter.—No—I must keep to my own style & go on in my own Way."

After *Emma* was published, Jane decided it was time to settle some old business. She asked Henry to buy back the copyright to *Susan* from Richard Crosby, the publisher who had purchased it thirteen years earlier. Once the transaction was complete, Henry had the great pleasure of telling Crosby that Susan was written by the author of the popular and successful novels *Sense and Sensibility* and *Pride and Prejudice*.

Reviews of *Emma* were numerous and excellent. One critic admitted that he had liked the book so much that it had kept him up at night. In an unsigned review, the respected writer Sir Walter Scott praised *Emma* as the best of the new style of novel that examined everyday life. He praised the author's realistic characters and her knowledge of the world.

SUFFERING

As Jane celebrated the success of *Emma,* Henry was experiencing serious financial problems. In March, his bank collapsed, and he lost all his money. His brother Charles had invested heavily in Henry's bank and also suffered major losses. Charles and Henry could no longer help support their mother and sisters.

Jane worked even harder to finish her current project, a novel she called "The Eliots." For the first time, Jane created an older heroine, Anne Eliot. Anne's older friend and neighbor, Lady Russell, talks her out of marrying Captain Wentworth because he is too poor. Anne breaks her engagement, even though she loves Wentworth. "She was persuaded to believe a wrong thing—indiscreet, improper, hardly capable of success . . . . She did not blame Lady Russell, she did not blame herself for having been guided by her; but she felt that were any young person, in similar circumstances, to apply to her for counsel, they would never receive any of such certain immediate wretchedness, such uncertain future good."

Wentworth goes on to make his fortune, and years later, the two find themselves in the same social circles again. In "The Eliots" (later titled *Persuasion*), Jane gave Anne what she never had herself—a second chance at love. "I offer myself to you again with a heart even more your own, than when you almost broke it eight years ago," Captain Wentworth tells Anne at the end of the novel. "I have loved none but you. For you alone I think and plan."

"The Eliots" progressed slowly because Jane was feeling ill. She had pain in her back, was feverish, and had trouble sleeping. She had also been busy entertaining visitors at Chawton and needed rest and quiet time alone to write. "Composition seems to me Impossible, with a head full of Joints of Mutton & doses of rhubarb," she wrote to Cassandra.

In May 1816, Jane and Cassandra traveled to the town of Cheltenham in hopes that the spa waters there might cure Jane's ailments. On the way to Cheltenham, they stopped at Steventon for the day. Their niece Caroline noticed that Jane seemed to act strangely. "Aunt Jane went over the old places, and recalled old recollections associated with them, in a very particular manner—looked at them, as if she never expected to see them again," Caroline later wrote.

By September, Jane insisted that she was feeling better. "My Back has given me scarcely any pain for many days," she wrote to Cassandra.

The new year seemed to bring the promise of improved health. Jane felt well enough to begin a new novel, writing twelve chapters in three months. But illness was on her mind—the novel, tentatively titled *The Brothers,* was set in seaside health resorts.

Jane also continued her regular correspondence. She often hid her illness behind jokes and chatty gossip. To her niece Caroline, Jane wrote, "*I* feel myself getting stronger than I was half a year ago & can so perfectly well walk to Alton, *or* back again, without the slightest fatigue that I hope to be able to do both when Summer comes."

Cheered by Jane's letter, Caroline was shocked by her aunt's condition when she saw her in March 1817. "She was very pale—her voice was weak and low. There was about her, a general appearance of . . . suffering," she said.

For several weeks, Jane had been unable "to write anything that was not absolutely necessary." By March, she had set aside *The Brothers*, unfinished. She suffered from fever, pain in her knees, and a complexion that shifted between "black & white & every wrong colour." Doctors could do little to help her. Jane was probably suffering from either a type of cancer or an illness called Addison's disease, which affects the kidneys.

Although Jane downplayed her illness, she must have known she was dying. In April she wrote her will, leaving small gifts to Henry and his housekeeper and everything else "to my dearest Sister Cassandra."

EPILOGUE

Unable to treat Jane's advancing illness, her doctor suggested that Cassandra take her to see Dr. Lyford in Winchester. In late May, Cassandra and Henry moved Jane to Winchester, fifteen miles from Chawton. They settled into a comfortable house on College Street.

Between May and July, Jane's condition worsened, improved, then worsened again. Dr. Lyford could only try to ease some of her pain. Sometimes Jane was strong enough to spend the day on the sofa. She tried to convince her family and friends that she was improving. "I am gaining strength very fast. I am now out of bed from 9 in the morng [sic] to 10 at night," she wrote to James Edward.

In the last stages of illness, Jane wrote several letters. She was comforted by visitors, including her brother Charles, her sister-in-law Mary Lloyd Austen, and Edward's sons. "If ever you are ill, may you be as tenderly nursed as I have been," she told them.

On July 15, Jane felt well enough to dictate a poem about the Winchester horse race. But that night, she "fell away" and slept for most of the next two days. During the last hours of her life, she seemed to be in pain, but she could not describe what she felt.

"When I asked her if there was any thing she wanted, her answer was she wanted nothing but death," Cassandra wrote.

Cassandra stayed by Jane's bed, cradling her head in her lap. In the early morning of July 18, 1817, forty-one-year-old Jane died in Cassandra's arms.

"I *have* lost a treasure, such a Sister, such a friend as never can have been surpassed," Cassandra wrote to Fanny Knight. "She was the sun of my life . . . the soother of every sorrow. I had not a thought concealed from her, & it is as if I had lost a part of myself."

Cassandra cut a few locks of Jane's hair and sent them and other mementos to Jane's nieces and friends. Most women in the early 1800s did not attend funerals, and Cassandra did not see Jane laid in her final resting ground in Winchester cathedral. But she stood at the window of the College Street house where Jane had died and "watched the little mournful procession the length of the Street & when it turned from my sight . . . I had lost her for ever."

Several papers reported Jane's death, and some identified her as an author. But in writing memorial lines for his sister's gravestone, Henry did not mention that Jane Austen was a writer whose novels had entertained a nation and pleased a prince.

Cassandra returned to Chawton, where Mrs. Austen and Martha Lloyd Austen were waiting for her. Henry, who had become a minister in Chawton after his business collapsed, was there as well. After Jane's death, Chawton Cottage lost much of its charm. "It was not only that the chief light in the house was quenched, but that the loss cast a shade over the spirits of the survivors," said Jane's nephew James Edward.

Perhaps her family's best tribute to Jane Austen was to publish her two remaining completed novels. *Susan* (renamed *Northanger Abbey*) and *Persuasion* (formerly "The Eliots") came out just six months after Jane's death. For the first time, Jane's books were published under her name. Henry wrote a short biography of the author as an introduction to *Persuasion*.

Although Jane had wanted Cassandra to determine the fate of her writings, Henry, accustomed to acting on Jane's behalf, continued to represent her work. In 1832 he persuaded Cassandra to sell the copyright to five of Jane's novels. The next year, the first edition of the collected works of Jane Austen appeared.

Cassandra continued to live at Chawton. She celebrated her sister's life and preserved her manuscripts and belongings. But a few years before her own death in 1845, Cassandra burned many of Jane's letters or took out portions of them. She did not want the world to read Jane's cruel jokes and harsh complaints or to know her resentments and disappointments.

Cassandra was not alone in her desire to immortalize her sister as gentle and kind. Henry also portrayed her as a pious, quiet spinster. Much later, James Edward recalled his aunt in a similar fashion in his *Memoir of Jane Austen.* For years people believed that Jane had led a narrow, dull life.

James Edward's somewhat sentimental biography,

published in 1870, rekindled the public's interest in Jane Austen. Although her novels were still in print, they had been overshadowed by the works of rising writers like Charles Dickens. In addition, times had changed. In the Victorian age, many readers preferred books that took a moral stance or examined social conditions.

James Edward's *Memoir* prompted the publication of some of Jane's earliest writings, including *Lady Susan* and *The Watsons*. In the years since then, Jane's letters and more of her early writings have been published, along with poems and family reminiscences.

Jane's literary style of domestic realism—lifelike portrayals of ordinary people—influenced other writers, including George Eliot (the pen name of Mary Ann Evans), Henry James, and E. M. Forster.

In the 1920s, Jane's stories were adapted into plays, and in the late 1930s, they were dramatized on the radio. The first movie version of a Jane Austen novel appeared in the 1940s. Her most popular novels—*Pride and Prejudice, Sense and Sensibility,* and *Emma*—have been adapted for the screen several times. In 1995 all three made it to the screen, and *People* magazine named Jane Austen one of the twenty-five most interesting people of the year. In the year 2000, 225 years after Jane's birth, a movie version of *Mansfield Park* was released.

Jane's enduring popularity is a reflection of her skill as a writer. She created lively characters and witty dialogue to champion individualism. As a social critic, Jane skillfully used irony—from sarcasm to understatement—to criticize social pretensions and false values. Her themes of love and marriage are timeless, and her observations of human nature are precise.

One only has to look to Jane's fiction to understand what she wanted to accomplish in her books: "I hope I never ridicule what is wise and good," Elizabeth Bennet declares in *Pride and Prejudice*. "Follies and nonsense, whims and inconsistencies *do* divert me . . . and I laugh at them whenever I can."

SOURCES

8 James Edward Austen-Leigh, *Memoir of Jane Austen* (London: Oxford University Press, 1926), 1–2.

8–9 Deirdre Le Faye, ed., *Jane Austen's Letters*, 3rd ed. (Oxford and New York: Oxford University Press, 1995), 323.

10 Valerie Grosvenor Myer, *Jane Austen: Obstinate Heart: A Biography* (New York: Arcade Publishing, Inc., 1997), 10.

11 William Austen-Leigh and Richard Arthur Austen-Leigh, *Jane Austen: Her Life and Letters: A Family Record*, 2nd ed. (New York: Russell and Russell, 1965), 21.

15–16 James Edward Austen-Leigh, 16.

16 Janet Todd, *The Sign of Angellica: Women, Writing, and Fiction, 1660–1800* (New York: Columbia University Press, 1989), 119.

17 Juliana-Susannah Seymour, *On the Management and Education of Children, a Series of Letters Written to a Niece* (London: R. Baldwin, 1754), 113–114.

19 Henry Austen, "Biographical Notice of the Author," in *Persuasion* by Jane Austen (London: Penguin Classics, 1985), 33.

20 David Nokes, *Jane Austen: A Life* (Los Angeles: University of California Press, 1997), 41.

24 John Halperin, "Unengaged Laughter: Jane Austen's Juvenilia," in *Jane Austen's Beginnings: The Juvenilia and Lady Susan*, ed. J. David Grey (Ann Arbor, MI: UMI Research Press, 1989), 32.

24 Deborah J. Knuth, "Friendship in Jane Austen's Juvenilia and *Lady Susan*," in *Jane Austen's Beginnings: The Juvenilia and Lady Susan*, ed. J. David Grey, (Ann Arbor, MI: UMI Research Press, 1989), 97–98.

25 Sir Egerton Brydges, *The Autobiography, Times, Opinions, and Contempories of Sir Egerton Brydges, in Two Volumes* (London: Chochrane and M'Crone, 1734), 41.

26 Deirdre Le Faye, ed., *Jane Austen: A Family Record* (London: British Library, 1989), 61.

28 Ellen E. Martin, "The Madness of Jane Austen: Metonymic

Style and Literature's Resistance to Interpretation," in *Jane Austen's Beginnings: The Juvenilia and Lady Susan,* ed. J. David Grey (Ann Arbor, MI: UMI Research Press, 1989), 86.

30 Le Faye, *Jane Austen: A Family Record,* 66.

30 Meenakshi Mukherjee, *Women Writers: Jane Austen* (New York: St. Martin's Press, 1991), 8.

31 Claire Tomalin, *Jane Austen: A Life* (New York: Alfred A. Knopf, 1997), 62.

31 Ibid., 67.

34 Jane Austen, *The History of England: From the Reign of Henry the 4th to the Death of Charles the 1st* (Chapel Hill, NC: Algonquin Books of Chapel Hill, 1993), ix.

34 Ibid., 37.

35 Ibid., 38.

35 Ibid., 39.

35 Ibid., 41.

36 Joan Rees, *Jane Austen: Woman and Writer* (New York: St. Martin's Press, 1976), 32.

37 James Edward Austen-Leigh, 87.

37 Henry Austen, 31.

39 Le Faye, *Jane Austen's Letters,* 61.

39 Ibid., 156.

39–40 Ibid., 61.

40 Le Faye, *Jane Austen: A Family Record,* 251.

41 Henry Austen, 33.

43 Le Faye, *Jane Austen: A Family Record,* 83.

45 James Edward Austen-Leigh, 17.

47 Le Faye, *Jane Austen's Letters,* 1.

47 Ibid.

47 Ibid., 4.

48 Ibid., 3.

48 Ibid., 4.

49 Jane Austen, *Pride and Prejudice* (Cambridge, MA: The Riverside Press, 1959), 83.

49 Le Faye, *Jane Austen's Letters,* 201.

50 George Holbert Tucker, *A Goodly Heritage: A History of Jane Austen's Family* (Manchester, England: Carcanet New Press, 1983), 159.

51 Le Faye, *Jane Austen: A Family Record*, 95.
51 Le Faye, *Jane Austen's Letters*, 13.
54 Ibid., 28.
55 Ibid., 20.
55 Ibid., 22.
55 Ibid., 18.
56 Ibid., 35.
57 Ibid., 17.
57 Ibid., 68.
58 Ibid.
58 Ibid., 22.
59 Ibid., 26.
59 Ibid., 31.
59 Ibid.
60 Jane Austen, *Northanger Abbey* (New York: New American Library, 1980), 90.
60 Ibid., 143–44.
61 Le Faye, *Jane Austen's Letters*, 44.
63 Ibid., 51.
63 Ibid., 57.
64 Le Faye, *Jane Austen: A Family Record*, 111.
64 Le Faye, *Jane Austen's Letters*, 68.
65 Ibid., 83.
65 Ibid., 85–86.
65 Ibid., 84, 88.
65 Ibid., 90.
67 Ibid., 159.
68 William Austen-Leigh and Richard Arthur Austen-Leigh, 93.
69 Le Faye, *Jane Austen's Letters*, 96.
71 Ibid., 174.
71 Ibid., 175.
71 Ibid., 332.
73 Le Faye, *Jane Austen's Letters*, 156.
73 Ibid., 178.
75 Ibid., 294.
75–76 Caroline Austen, *My Aunt Jane Austen: A Memoir* (London: The Jane Austen Society, 1952), 5, 10.
77 James Edward Austen-Leigh, 102.

77 Ibid.
79 Henry Austen, 31.
80 Le Faye, *Jane Austen's Letters,* 182.
81 Le Faye, *Jane Austen: A Family Record,* 168.
81 Le Faye, *Jane Austen's Letters,* 201.
81 Ibid.
82 Ibid.
83 Ibid., 217.
83 Ibid., 221.
83 John Halperin, "Nineteenth-Century Criticisms of Austen's Novels," in *Readings on Jane Austen,* ed. David Bender et al. (San Diego: Greenhaven Press, 1997), 53.
84 Le Faye, *Jane Austen: A Family Record,* 184.
84 Le Faye, *Jane Austen's Letters,* 239.
85 David Selwyn, ed., *The Poetry of Jane Austen and the Austen Family* (Iowa City, IA: University of Iowa Press in association with the Jane Austen Society, 1997), 61.
86 Le Faye, *Jane Austen's Letters,* 198.
86 Caroline Austen, 10.
86 Le Faye, *Jane Austen's Letters,* 319.
87 Ibid., 275.
89 James Edward Austen-Leigh, 157.
89 Jane Austen, *Emma* (London: Pan Books, 1969), 19.
89 Ibid., 25.
90 Ibid., 54.
90 R. W. Chapman, *Jane Austen: Facts and Problems* (Oxford: Clarendon Press, 1948), 86.
90 Jane Austen, *Plan of a Novel According to Hints by Various Quarters, by Jane Austen, With Opinions on* Mansfield Park *and* Emma *Collected and Transcribed by Her* (London: Oxford University Press, 1972), 14.
92 Le Faye, *Jane Austen's Letters,* 312.
93 Jane Austen, *Persuasion* (London: Penguin Books, 1965), 57–58.
93 Ibid., 240.
94 Le Faye, *Jane Austen's Letters,* 321.
94 Caroline Austen, 14.
94 Le Faye, *Jane Austen's Letters,* 320.
94 Ibid., 326.

95 Caroline Austen, 15.

95 Le Faye, *Jane Austen's Letters,* 338.

95 Ibid., 335.

95 Ibid., 339.

96 Ibid., 342.

96 Ibid.

96 Ibid., 344.

97 Ibid.

97 Ibid., 347.

97–98 Henry Austen, 33.

100 Jane Austen, *Pride and Prejudice,* 42.

SELECTED BIBLIOGRAPHY

Austen, Caroline. *My Aunt Jane Austen: A Memoir.* London: The Jane Austen Society, 1952.

Austen, Henry. "Biographical Notice of the Author." In *Persuasion* by Jane Austen. London: Penguin Classics, 1985.

Austen-Leigh, Emma. *Jane Austen and Steventon.* 2nd edition. London: Spottiswoode, Ballantyne and Co., Ltd., 1937.

Austen-Leigh, James Edward. *Memoir of Jane Austen.* London: Oxford University Press, 1926.

Austen-Leigh, Richard Arthur, ed. *Austen Papers: 1704–1856.* London: Spottiswoode, Ballantyne and Co., Ltd., 1942.

Austen-Leigh, William, and Richard Arthur Austen-Leigh. *Jane Austen: Her Life and Letters: A Family Record.* 2nd edition. New York: Russell and Russell, 1965.

Austen-Leigh, William, and Richard Arthur Austen-Leigh, with Deirdre Le Faye. *Jane Austen: A Family Record.* Boston: G. K. Hall and Co., 1989.

Craik, W. A. *Jane Austen in Her Time.* London: Thomas Nelson and Sons, Ltd., 1969.

Fyson, Nance Lui. *Growing up in the Eighteenth Century.* London: B. T. Batsford, Ltd., 1977.

Hickman, Peggy. *A Jane Austen Household Book with Martha Lloyd's Recipes.* London: David and Charles, 1977.

Hill, Constance. *Jane Austen: Her Home and Her Friends.* London: John Lane, 1901.

Hughes-Hallett, Penelope, ed. *Jane Austen: "My Dear Cassandra."* London: Collins and Brown, 1990.

Lane, Maggie. *Jane Austen's England.* New York: St. Martin's Press, 1986.

Laski, Marghanita. *Jane Austen and Her World.* New York: Viking Press, 1972.

Le Faye, Deirdre, ed. *Jane Austen's Letters.* 3rd edition. Oxford and New York: Oxford University Press, 1995.

Modert, Jo. "Letters/Correspondence." In *The Jane Austen Companion,* edited by J. David Grey. New York: Macmillan Publishing Company, 1986.

Mukherjee, Meenakshi. *Women Writers: Jane Austen.* New York: St. Martin's Press, 1991.

Myer, Valerie Grosvenor. *Jane Austen: Obstinate Heart: A Biography.* New York: Arcade Publishing, Inc., 1997.

Nicolson, Nigel. *The World of Jane Austen.* London: Phoenix Illustrated Orion Publishing Group, 1997.

Nokes, David. *Jane Austen: A Life.* Los Angeles: University of California Press, 1997.

Pool, Daniel. *What Jane Austen Ate and Charles Dickens Knew: From Fox Hunting to Whist—the Facts of Daily Life in Nineteenth-Century England.* New York: Simon and Schuster, 1993.

Poplawksi, Paul. *A Jane Austen Encyclopedia.* Westport, CT: Greenwood Press, 1998.

Rees, Joan. *Jane Austen: Woman and Writer.* New York: St. Martin's Press, 1976.

Tomalin, Claire. *Jane Austen: A Life.* New York: Alfred A. Knopf, 1997.

Tucker, George Holbert. *A Goodly Heritage: A History of Jane Austen's Family.* Manchester, England: Carcanet New Press, 1983.

———. *Jane Austen the Woman: Some Biographical Insights.* New York: St. Martin's Press, 1994.

Weldon, Fay. "England in Austen's Time." In *Readings on Jane Austen,* edited by David Bender et al. San Diego: Greenhaven Press, 1997.

Published Works by Jane Austen

The Beautifull Cassandra	*Northanger Abbey*
The Brothers	*Opinions of Mansfield Park*
Emma	*Persuasion*
Henry and Eliza	*Pride and Prejudice*
The History of England	*Sense and Sensibility*
Lady Susan	*Susan*
Love and Freindship	*The Watsons*
Mansfield Park	

INDEX

OTHER TITLES FROM LERNER AND A&E®:

Arthur Ashe

Bill Gates

Bruce Lee

Carl Sagan

Chief Crazy Horse

Christopher Reeve

Edgar Allan Poe

Eleanor Roosevelt

George Lucas

Gloria Estefan

Jack London

Jacques Cousteau

Jesse Owens

Jesse Ventura

Jimi Hendrix

John Glenn

Latin Sensations

Legends of Dracula

Legends of Santa Claus

Louisa May Alcott

Madeleine Albright

Mark Twain

Maya Angelou

Mohandas Gandhi

Mother Teresa

Nelson Mandela

Princess Diana

Queen Cleopatra

Queen Latifah

Rosie O'Donnell

Saint Joan of Arc

Thurgood Marshall

Wilma Rudolph

Women in Space

Women of the Wild West

ABOUT THE AUTHOR

Amy Ruth is a writer in Williamsburg, Virginia, where she lives with her husband, writer and photographer Jim Meisner Jr., and their chocolate lab puppy, Jane Austen.

AUTHOR ACKNOWLEDGMENTS

Permission to quote from *Jane Austen's Letters* (3rd Edition, collected and edited by Deirdre Le Faye, published by Oxford University Press, 1995) granted by Oxford University Press.

PHOTO ACKNOWLEDGMENTS

North Wind Picture Archives, pp. 2, 22, 32, 38, 42, 74; Corbis: (© Michael Busselle) p. 6, (© Historical Picture Archive) p. 14, (© Philadelphia Museum of Art) p. 28, (© Bettman) p. 62; Mrs. E. Fowler, pp. 11, 12; Jane Austen Memorial Trust, pp. 18, 30; Hamlyn Group, Sally Chappell, p. 20; Goeff Goode Pictures, p. 26; Institution of Civil Engineers/Mary Evans Picture Library, p. 27; J. Butler-Kearney, p. 35; J. G. Lefroy, p. 48; Mansell Collection/TimePix, pp. 52, 72; from *The History and Topographical Survey of the County of Kent* by E. Hasted, 1799, p. 54; Jane Austen Memorial Trust and J. Butler-Kearney, pp. 70, 86; from *Sense and Sensibility*, T. Egerton, Whitehall, London, 1811, p. 78; Giraudon/Art Resource, NY, p. 82; Great Grandsons of Admiral Sir Frances Austen, p. 87; (© Hulton Getty/Liaison Agency, Inc., p. 88; Royal Library, Windsor Castle, p. 91; Jim Meisner, Jr., p. 112.
Front cover photo courtesy of Henry Rice/Mary Evans Picture Library.
Back cover photo courtesy of Mary Evans Picture Library.